Grieving as a Woman

Grieving as a Woman

Moving Through Life's Many Losses

Kass P. Dotterweich

With a Foreword by
Evelina Mendoza-Mabini, M.D.

Abbey Press

© 1998 by Kass P. Dotterweich
Published by One Caring Place
Abbey Press
St. Meinrad, Indiana 47577

Library of Congress Catalog Number
97-78045

ISBN 0-87029-310-9

Printed in the United States of America

For
Margaret,
Sheila,
Christine,
and
Bess

And with gratitude to all those women
who have shared
their sacred stories
with me

TABLE OF CONTENTS

FOREWORD

Longfellow wrote, "There is no grief like the grief that does not speak." This simple truth came home to me through a six-year-old boy whose dog was hit by a car while he was away visiting his grandmother. The family rallied around the boy by giving him a new puppy right away and by continuously praising him for being a "big, brave boy."

Soon, however, he began to pick fights at school. And his mother could not understand why he kept coming down with a cold several times a month.

After I had examined him, I asked his mother if she would leave the room for a while. The little boy ran to a corner and refused to look at me. I waited. Finally, after a long silence, I heard a whimper. It slowly grew to loud sobbing. His mother hurriedly opened the door and asked him why he was crying.

He turned to her and blurted out, "Because I'm not done yet!"

~

I will always be grateful to Kass Dotterweich for writing this book. She has given all women—and the men in their lives, too—an excellent guide for the mysterious journey known as grief. It is a book written by, to, for, and about women experiencing grief not in an attempt to exclude men—indeed, we women grieve with and for men all the time—but rather to address an important need. In spite of—and in part because of—the manifold, nurturing roles that women play, it is too often the case that a woman's own need to grieve well is the last need to be attended to. "Moms aren't allowed to get sick," I often hear while attending to a mother's sick child. "And busy women aren't allowed to grieve," one could add.

Grieving is a health issue as well as an emotional and spiritual one. Grief brings great stress, which, if not properly attended to, puts a person at risk for serious illness. Studies have shown that the ability of the body to combat infection decreases dramatically during periods of intense psychological suffering. Feelings associated with grief sift through the pathways of the brain and translate into physical symptoms such as headaches, backaches, and joint pain. During periods of intense grief, a person tends to neglect such important health habits as good nutrition, exercise, hygiene, and rest, thereby putting further stress on the body. It can be a vicious cycle.

Fortunately, Kass Dotterweich has given us a tool to break the cycle of unhealthy grieving. Her book is filled with wisdom, and written in language and images that will speak directly to the deepest recesses of a woman's soul. As she has written elsewhere, "When we are able to grieve well as women, we will look at the tapestry of our lives and see the precious threads of loss and grief, and we will recognize the fabric as our own. We will see how loss gave way to gain, death gave way to life, and pain gave way to peace."

May Kass's book help you find your way on the road from loss to gain, death to life, pain to peace. Savor this book, for it is filled with nourishing nuggets of wisdom and insight—food for the journey ahead. It is the way of all women—indeed, the way of all the earth.

Evelina Mendoza-Mabini, M.D.
Hales Corners, Wisconsin

Why "Grieving as a Woman"?

In the dark and desolate hours of early morning, August 31, 1997, 36-year-old Diana Spencer, Princess of Wales, was killed in a violent automobile accident—and the entire world grieved. Gone from our fantasies, our news clips, our curious ponderings, was "England's Rose," as Elton John memorialized her in an adaptation of his song "Candle in the Wind." Whether or not you were a fan of Princess Di, followed her life events, or were aware of her worldwide efforts to relieve some of life's greatest sufferings, you at least *knew of* Princess Di—and you were part of the hush that settled over much of the human race as news of her death spread around the world.

Death is part of life. It visits us with a force unlike any other human experience, and on the other side of our grief, life as we knew it is changed forever.

Princess Di's death, violent and shocking, brought this reality to light for millions of mourners in the days, weeks, and months after the tragedy. Even today, and for decades to come, there will be those who weep at her memory—and at the void that has been left in the wake of her death. That is the power of death and that is the essence of grief.

But why a book especially for women on the experience of grief?

Very simply, there is very little popular reading material available on how women grieve. In another recent writing assignment I did on women and grief, I combed metropolitan libraries and the shelves of major bookstore chains looking for work *by* women *for* women on what and how we grieve. I found nothing.

Surprised with that simple piece of "research," I decided to use my own wealth of resources to create a gentle, embracing, and healing work that will support women in all the ways we grieve. And what are those resources? The rich experiences of my sisterhood: women willing to share their stories of what they grieve, why they grieve, and how they grieve. Sure, for the deep, psychological facts and data on women and grief, perhaps we need studies, tests, charts, and "serious" research. But the wisdom of the heart, our greatest strength, is already ours—available to each of us from within.

Grieving as a Woman

Grief is a universal experience. Human beings of every culture experience grief as a result of loss; loss and grief are inevitable. There are, in fact, moments of loss and grief for each of us every day of our lives.

But the journey of grief for a woman, the work surrounding grief for a woman, and the passage through grief for a woman all have unique characteristics. The wonder and splendor of our nature as women leave us oriented in the world with unique vision, wisdom, strength, and promise; they equip us for mystery—and grief is many things, including mystery.

Women grieve with their bodies and their hearts—together. So we begin with our unique and wondrous body. As women we come into the world wombed creatures; whether that vessel issues physical life or spirit life or both, our female body enters the world bearing the same characteristics of the dark, moist, and life-full chamber that gave shape to our own body. Because of that *mystery* alone, we are part of a continuous chord of potential life. We are gifted in special ways, ways that set us out on life with the tools we need for the countless, unknown marvels we will encounter—including the inevitable experience of grief. We may not know, especially in the midst of savage pain, that we are visionaries, sages, Amazons, and prophets. But we are, indeed.

We also rely on our emotions—the world of the

heart—to name our life experiences. We *feel* our way through a world that is structured around logic and analytical thinking. Throughout the ages, we have survived because our feelings and our emotions have helped us find meaning where thinking simply could not penetrate. And when the pain of grief slices deep into our hearts, there is no thinking; there is only that which we *feel*.

Thus, we grieve—deeply, fully—with our bodies and with our emotions. This sets us apart and leaves us acutely aware of the long and embracing arms of grief. Physically and emotionally, we know that grief—sound, solid, healthy grief—seeps out far beyond the shores of death, and together, we can learn to grieve well all that we experience as loss.

∼

This book is divided into three parts. Part I looks at the overall experience of grief. Chapter One introduces grief as a life-long process. Using the analogy of birth, we see that grief is actually an experience we've known throughout our entire life—starting with our own birth. We wander through the confusion of "naming" our grief and find ourselves at a starting point from which we can begin the journey of grieving well.

Part II explores the specific losses we grieve. Chapter Two visits with the "grandmother" of all grief: death. We will learn the importance of grieving with a passion, and we will wander along those sacred pieces that help us get through our grief and make us strong for a life-giving future.

Chapter Three delves into the emotions we experience when we grieve changes in our significant relationships. We learn to re-name our "selves" in this process, find courage in the fact that we never really "let go," and face the souring threat of bitterness that can rob of us the vital energy we need for healing.

Chapter Four gives us permission to grieve that which our culture would have us ignore: the loss of precious *possessions*. We gain respect for "attachment" and learn how to carve out our own respect for our grief. Along the way, we take a look at those "security blankets" that we can rely on to carry us along our journey.

Part III serves as a basic collection of specific directions that you can select and modify to fit your unique needs while you grieve. Chapter Five offers practical suggestions for grieving well, including certain cautions, comments about the role of humor, and insights about the process of change.

Chapter Six offers spiritual suggestions for grieving well, including directions for ritual, blessing your memories, and exploring the healing environment of a faith community. It is followed by a brief, personal Postscript.

At the end of the book, you will find a few suggestions for further reading that will support you as you grieve in your own way and time.

~

All This as a Woman

Throughout the text you will be given opportunities to process the material and explore your own experience. "All This as a Woman" offers directions and questions that help you focus attention on your own thoughts, feelings, and memories.

Decide for yourself how these sections best support your needs at this time. If a quiet time of reflection leads you to helpful insights, consider adding atmosphere like music, candles, and incense. Many women find journaling to be a challenging means of self-exploration. "All This as a Woman" offers excellent points of departure. You may want to consider sharing these sections with a spiritual director, prayer partner, or women's support group. The experiences of other women inevitably enrich and broaden our own.

Keep in mind that your grief is uniquely yours. No one can define it for you or do the grief work for you. You must do this yourself—and ultimately, you're the one who can best determine what constitutes your own healthy grieving. "All This as a Woman" is only a potential tool. You will find no miracles nestled there, no quick fixes, no answers—just more of you. And *you* are capable of entering this pain, of bringing your woman wisdom to its mysteries, of finding peace.

∼

Pieces of Grief

A line drawing of a graceful little cherub nestled in the lower corner of the page of the guest registration book: a fitting touch. After signing my name, I turned for one last blessing glance at my friend, Millie. She stood where I had left her only moments earlier, where I had hugged her and fumbled through some tearful and painful words of condolence. On her hip, Millie bounced her 14-month-old son, Andrew—while she stared down into the casket of Andrew's twin brother, Aaron, a victim of Sudden Infant Death Syndrome. My eyes spilled tears, my breathing became shallow and sharp—and I headed for the nearest exit.

Crossing the parking lot to my car, I saw Sandy, a co-worker. After we exchanged comments about the tragedy of Aaron's death and the family's grief, Sandy told me her news: her husband had "gotten the job," and she and her family would soon relocate to the West Coast. I knew this was one of those good news/bad news situations for Sandy, and I promised myself that I'd organize a little going-away affair at the office for her before she left.

On my way home, I stopped to pick up a few grocery items and chanced to meet Terry, leader of our women's prayer group. Her daughter had failed, once again, to pass the bar exam—the young woman's last opportunity to become the attorney she had long dreamed of being.

When I arrived home, tired and distressed from a day too full of the raw realities of life, I found my daughter Christine curled up in a pain-stricken fetal position on the living room couch. She often baby-sat for Andrew and Aaron, and she was, perhaps for the first time in her innocent 13 years of life, facing immense emotional pain. I quietly set down my parcels, knelt down on the floor beside the couch, and helplessly draped my own body across the sobbing body of my beloved child. Did I think I could somehow be a protective blanket between her and an inevitable mystery of life: loss and grief?

In the short span of an hour, I saw, heard, touched, and emotionally felt the many dimensions of women enduring loss and walking through inevitable grief. Millie: a woman grieving the loss of her precious son. Millie would eventually have to go home to an empty crib, to silent toys, to size-2 clothes that would never again be needed. Through endless hours of grief, Millie would carry a haunting concern for Andrew's welfare, and possibly her own guilt at having somehow failed to protect her child.

Sandy: a woman grieving the loss of home. Sandy would soon begin to gather boxes for "packing," decline invitations for future social events, and think in terms of "one last time." She would leave parents, siblings, friends, and a community she'd known for 31 years, to enter an unfamiliar world where new connections would have to be forged. She would soon look back over her shoulder at the receding countryside that had been home her entire life.

Terry: a woman grieving for and with her child in the loss of a dream. Terry would face her daughter's disappointment and would open her arms to cradle the lost dream. She would go deep into her own strength to find just the right support for her grieving child. A cup of tea nearby, she would spend hours with her daughter, late into the night, offering encouragement, exploring options, and recreating hope with and for her child. She would remember her own failures, and hurt for her daughter, who would ultimately have to find her own way back to self-confidence and purpose.

Christine: a young woman grieving for a baby-friend—and a life of innocence. Christine would soon sleep, but something of the new day would bring young Aaron back to mind: the face of her own little brother, the laughter of a neighborhood child, the invitation to the twins' first birthday party peeking out from a layer of clutter on her bedroom dresser. In time, Millie would call to see if Christine could baby-sit for Andrew, and Christine would enter the very environment in which she had so sweetly and maternally cared for Aaron in his parents' absence.

Me: a woman carrying a piece of grief with and for each of these women, a sister to each one in a common universe of woman strength and wisdom. I would come face to face again with each of these women in the near future. I would prepare a relish tray to take to Millie's home the day of the funeral—just a little something to help lighten the cooking load for the gathered family. I would plan a small going-away luncheon for Sandy—just a little surprise thing to provide her with warm memories as the miles took her further and further from "home." I would see Terry when we next gathered for prayer, and would reach out to her with gentle words—just a heart-touch to say "I care." And Christine: Before the pain became a familiar part of her life, I would dry her moist cheeks and rock her in my arms in every room of the house, every hour of the day—just a little security in the midst of some of life's most profound mysteries: loss and grief.

Each of us was *grieving as a woman*.

PART I

The Life-Long Process of Grief

*Loss grew
as you did,
without your
consent.*

ANNIE DILLARD

CHAPTER ONE

A Loss by Any Other Name: Grief as Part of Life

Grief is a natural experience of life, a response to the realities of being human. It is unavoidable, and involves a flush of emotions that range from mild, perhaps even unnoticed, to dramatic and life altering.

The seeds of grief take form in the womb, just as the human body does. The very environment of the womb sets up the inevitable experience of grief—which is first experienced in our own birth.

Imagine for a moment the wondrous home of the womb. After all, we were there, in that space, for a long time. We may have no conscious recall of that experience, but our body memory still carries an awareness of that first home. There, in that secure and comfortable world, we were kept warm, moist, fed, and breathing; every body function was natural, spontaneous. We became familiar with the feel of our home and the constant sounds of Mother's voice and heartbeat. We developed and grew with a tremendous sense of Mother's life rhythms, and took them on as our own; we knew nothing else and needed nothing else.

Then, at a time mysteriously determined to be uniquely ours, the world we knew and felt secure in began to change, to recede. It started with unfamiliar movements that seemed beyond our control. We became aware of a pressure that seemed to have a life of its own, that pulled and pushed on us regardless of our own infant will. We were no longer free to tumble and stretch with abandon, but rather were squeezed from every side. Mother's heartbeat changed and her familiar rhythm was gone, replaced by something urgent and demanding. Like it or not, we were forced into the birth canal to struggle— along with Mother—to reach some unknown destination.

At that point in the drama, we began to grieve. What was familiar and comfortable in the womb world—what we "knew"—was left behind as we entered the unfamiliar and the initially uncomfortable. We were confused, angry, vulnerable: all characteristics of grief. We no longer knew what to expect, what to count on. In fact, we didn't even know who we were—what we were. In the womb, we had been autonomous in a world that conformed to our being.

In the birth process, we lost that autonomy and became something, someone else—and would spend our lives trying to figure out what and who that something and someone else is. That first moment of air drawn into our lungs was a "never-before" experience that told us nothing would ever be the same.

Sound, for example, had changed. It took on an entirely new dimension on the other side of birth. It was sharp, often abrasive, and ever-changing. Even Mother's voice was different, and her heartbeat wasn't as close and constant. Within seconds, we began to sense that sound served a purpose—and that we would have to learn that purpose and use it if we were to survive in this new place.

Our vision, too, was different. What was dark and shadowy became flooded with hues of light. We couldn't name that light, but we knew how to respond to it. We squinted, turned our heads, and closed our eyes to adjust to visuals over which we had absolutely no control. Again, we sensed that this light served a purpose and that we would have to adjust to it if we were to see our way in this new place.

The sense of touch was different. Through the walls of the womb, Mother's caress was distant but recognizable. The occasional probe of an unfamiliar touch was disturbing, but passing and tolerable. After the journey of birth, Mother's touch was direct—sometimes cold, sometimes warm; sometimes soothing, sometimes disturbing. And there were other touches. Air on the surface of our skin made us squirm to find a balance between things we would someday know as warmth and cold. Pressures on the surface of our skin, something we would know as clothing, completely enfolded us as a simulation of that familiar snug place we had just left behind.

We learn, many years later, that the savage movement from pre-birth through birth to life was, literally, the opportunity of a lifetime. We were destined to know a fuller life, one sprinkled with the delights of the universe: a multitude of sense experiences, expanses of the mind, rich encounters with our Creator, and the splendid realities of emotional and physical love.

Ultimately, birth brought us into the first movements toward our own selfhood. Within the narrow confines of the womb, we never would have had an opportunity to enter the cathedral of life. The womb was only the vestibule of this cathedral; it wasn't "designed" to be the total experience of life. Had we clung to that secure space—as if we had any choice in the matter—we would have missed the marvelous gift that had been ours from before time became a human concept. Yet, we had to go by way of a deep and profound grief to reach the center of the cathedral of life. All our grief offers this same potential to life.

All This as a Woman

- *Imagine the womb-home you once knew. Visualize yourself as a precious being, fetally secure in that dark, moist, life-sustaining environment. What thoughts and feelings might you have had about the sights, sounds, and physical sensations of your world in that place?*
- *Imagine your journey toward birth. How did your womb-home change? Imagine what your fear would have been as everything you had grown to know and rely upon began to recede.*
- *Imagine your release from your mother's body. Let your body feel the first touch of human hands, of cloth, of cold and heat. Close your eyes for 60 seconds, and then open them again slowly, imagining your first encounter with light.*
- *Imagine yourself at six months of age. Feel the delight of your mother's touch, the taste of milk, the caress of water, the smell of your own body. Contrast your experience of life in those first moments after release from your mother's body to your experience of life at six months of age.*
- *Can you see how you've been through the journey of grief before, when you compare your experience today to the experience of being born?*

Grief As a Process of Change

Grief is not something we plan, like getting an education, buying a house, or taking a trip. Even when a lingering and terminal illness brings an expected death, we're never ready to grieve. Rather, grief moves in and, like a rude and unwelcome house guest, takes over and wreaks havoc. This havoc is called change.

The experience of grief is the savage awareness that life is *different* and that the change we know is extremely difficult. We might even use a simple formula to help us focus our journey through grief: grief = change. I recall my sister's comment at the death of our father: "Kass, nothing will ever be the same."

When we're ready to accept this reality, we've made a significant first step in our walk through grief. When we're ready to allow our imaginations to begin looking at the details of what we mean when we say, "Nothing will ever be the same," we've touched our feminine courage. We're ready to stretch, to let our hearts, souls, and lives expand to take in *the different*.

No, we won't actually *do* anything right away. We hurt too much; we're confused; we're tired. But we've opened the door to let change introduce itself—and that's the beginning.

The Saturday after Thanksgiving, Bonnie's sister told her she was filing for a divorce. Bonnie was heartbroken; she faced the death of a relationship that had brought her years of delight. Her mind flooded with memories of her sister's wedding day, of the anniversaries, of the family gatherings, of her niece's and nephew's births. And then, without realizing that she was already drawing on her own natural courage, her thoughts rushed ahead to the Christmas holidays: "How can the family celebrate with love—as a family—when it just won't be the same?" Through the months that followed, Bonnie was a tremendous support to her sister, and found her own way toward peace, all because she saw the immediate *change* in store for her entire family. She experienced anger and disappointment, she hurt for her family, she shed many tears. But her grief was wholesome because she named change. She did not ignore it or fight it. Bonnie's pain included what was different, and she grieved well.

The seasons—as they come on, develop into fullness, and fade away—tell us so much about the experience of grief as a response to change. The blush of summer, for example, surrounds us with rich greens, blossoms of every kind, sunshine-filled days, and willowy soft nights pulsing with the songs of crickets. Then, one morning, a sharp, crisp air sets off the alarm that sends us to the back of the closet for those long-stored sweaters and jackets. We take on the chores of harvest and enter the realities of autumn: her splendid colors, her friendly chill, her unique smells that generate a sense of "homewardness" and gratitude for the simple joys of a cup of soup. Then autumn fades, winter moves in, and we turn to those measures of self-care that help us adjust to and enjoy the new season. We cuddle into our woolies, keep the furnace in operating condition, and enter the celebrations of those ancient traditions known as "the holidays." Through the long and dormant months of winter, we don't cling to those discarded pages of the calendar—those summer and autumn days that simply will never return. Rather, we plan for that time when the earth will again be moist and pregnant, when we'll emerge from our cocoons of artificial warmth to embrace the natural warmth of spring.

We can no more hold off the changing seasons than we can hold off the changes we endure as a result of loss and grief. The difference is, we've *been through* the changing seasons. We know what to savor in the moment of any given season; we know what to anticipate, how to plan, how to cope—and how to hope. The mystery of grief is that *we don't know* any of this. We feel like we've lost the opportunity to savor moments, and we don't know how to anticipate, how to cope—or how to hope. We know only the pain of powerful and unfamiliar emotions, unplanned tomorrows, and change. This is grief.

All This as a Woman
- *How have you handled change in the past?*
- *Think back to the changes you've faced in recent years. Remember the grief that accompanied those changes.*
- *In your current experience, what must change as a result of the loss you face? Be as detailed and specific as possible.*
- *Will your past experiences—successful and unsuccessful—of coping with change help you adjust to the changes that your current loss brings?*

The Language of Woman Loss

Grieving as a woman has its own language. That language parallels the universal language of human grief. But because we are women, our use of the language has a unique character. We are, by nature, relational creatures. Be it another human being, a material object or physical environment, our own bodies, our memories, an isolated experience, we are in touch with our lives through the language of connection and relationship.

For example, we hear ourselves saying, "my grief." Grief is, after all, a self-centered experience, and women know that. Our very beings realize, as Anne Morrow Lindbergh says, "Grief can't be shared." In a broader context, of course, *self-centered* is one of those nasty, to-be-avoided, immature orientations that our culture—and probably our very upbringing—conditioned us to judge "unacceptable." But in our current experience of loss, and in grieving as a woman, we somehow know that *self-centered* is not only accurate but necessary. We know that this experience is ours: "This is my grief! It is about me as an individual. It is about my life." To claim it as mine is to begin naming exactly what one's grief is.

We also hear ourselves saying, "I'll never get over it." That's our language, a language that comes from our woman's body, gifted with a womb-bearing capacity for life. We are gifted with the ability to experience life as connected, all threads interrelating and integrating: yesterday connects to tomorrow in today. We will never "get over" this loss; we never "got over" the experience of birth. Regardless of how many calendar years have been turned over in the counting of our age, we know that the losses in the birth journey are never over. In the same way, we will not get over this loss; we will simply relate to it in a different way. And that, too, will change. We will relate to the loss differently in six months—and then differently again in a year, two years, three years.

When I returned to my father's grave two years after his death, I did not return as I had the first year—and that first year was different compared to the day we buried Dad. I was different. The eyes of my heart and soul looked on Dad's grave marker in a different way. I still grieved Dad's absence, but life had molded me further and the tears shed then were simply different. When I return next year, my tears will be different still—but never gone. Life is ongoing; grief is ongoing. Women know this well. Author Anne Finger completes this wisdom for us by turning it around: "Part of getting over it is knowing that you'll never get over it." Our acceptance of this leaves us well-equipped to name and direct our grief, for our own good and the good of others.

Naming: The Beginning of Good Grief

The story of the many faces of grief shared in the

Introduction involved a series of losses. Note, however, that I was not the woman who lost a child to death, nor the woman who lost her familiar world to build a new one over a thousand miles away. I was not the woman whose daughter lost her dream of becoming a lawyer, nor the young woman who lost an infant-friend. These women were gripped by the pain of first-level grief; their losses were directly personal and would wield tremendous and painful influence on their lives. My losses in all these encounters, on the other hand, were primarily second-level losses. I hurt for those I cared for as they faced the immediate pain of loss and grief.

This is naming our grief, and it begins with understanding our grief as either first-level grief or second-level grief; note that most of our first-level grief will carry with it second-level grief. My sister grieved my father's death, for example, as a first-level grief. But when she thought of her infant son growing up not knowing Granddad, she entered second-level grief. Once we name the grief by level, we then name its reality with the question, "Exactly what have I lost?"

Until we name our grief—the level as well as the specific loss—we remain unfocused, unable to get a grip on confusion, unable to regain a sense of direction in life, unable to step into our role in the experience. Neither you nor I, of course, can name or classify another's grief. But for the sake of understanding,

I chance to be so bold here as to offer a naming of the exact loss in the first-level grief for Millie, Sandy, Terry, and Christine.

Millie: Numb and broken, Millie stares down at the lifeless body of her child. She grieves, in addition to the loss of this precious human being, the loss of *a role*. Until three days earlier, she was the "mother of twins," the "mother of two," the "mother of *children*." With Aaron's death, her new role is "mother of Andrew," "mother of one," "mother of *a child*."

Sandy: Confused with her good news/bad news situation, Sandy grieves the loss of *security*. For over three decades, Sandy knew what home meant, and rooted her security in that meaning. With relocation, Sandy lost what was dear and familiar. She lost her secure sense of "home."

Terry: Facing her daughter's failure, Terry lost *status*. "My daughter the attorney" would not be part of her vocabulary. Hard as that will be, Terry must name that loss for herself before she can walk with her daughter toward another dream.

Christine: Her infant-friend will no longer delight her. Christine lost an avenue of *self-expression*. She lost a precious place to put the unique and budding joy of nurturing that she had lavished on Aaron.

This is the naming of first-level grief and the specific loss. To some degree, we grieve every day. I'm grieving from this morning's bad news: my furnace needs unexpected repairs—and the estimated cost is, frankly, shocking. I'm angry. I've taken care of the furnace; I've had it "inspected" and maintained with the coming of each winter. So what's this major repair? This isn't fair. I didn't do anything to cause this, I don't want this, and I don't know how I'm going to manage the added burden to the household budget. This is grief; in this case, I grieve the loss of financial resources. It may be a relatively minor experience of grief, but it's nonetheless a moment of first-level grief that, when named, gives me a better sense of why I feel the way I feel.

I recently named a second-level grief for myself when my 19-year-old son asked me to give a quick editorial look to his "paper for English Comp" before he handed it in. Without warning, I found myself grieving for my son: second-level grief. Of his father's and my divorce, he wrote:

> *The announcement of the divorce came as a shock to all of us, and we all left the room in pain and confusion. That evening was one of the coldest ever in my life. I felt numb, like I had died...*
>
> *My mom, younger sister, and I left everything behind in the house I grew up in except the clothes in my dresser and on my back. I left my friends during a day of school and that is where I knew I had to start all over...*
>
> *My mom knew my pain and confusion and helped me through it all and is still teaching me. I miss my father...*

My son's experience was not my experience of the divorce; our respective losses were—and are—first-level. But reading his paper late at night—trying to be an objective editor and not the author's mother—I shed tears for the pain my child had known and continues to know: this is second-level grief. Naming this over and over, for myself, has contributed to what my son so beautifully named: "helped me through it all and is still teaching me."

In the final analysis, of course, loss is a combination of first-level and second-level grief. Millie, Sandy, Terry, Christine, and I can tell you that as we experienced our own losses, we watched others and felt their pain, too. We always grieve, directly and indirectly, for ourselves and for others.

All This as a Woman

- *What is the pain you currently experience? Is it primarily a first-level grief or a second-level grief?*
- *Are you comfortable owning the grief? How does the phrase "my grief" sound and feel to you? Can you be self-centered enough to say "This is my grief"? If not, why?*
- *Can you name the grief? What, exactly, have you lost? Consider words like* role, security, pride, self-expression.
- *When you name your grief, does your sense of self seem to become clearer, stronger, or calmer? Do you have a better sense of what you can do for yourself? For others?*

PART II

The Many Faces of Grief

*Death will make
nonsense of
your hopes.*

THERESE DE LISIEUX

CHAPTER TWO

The Final Door: Grieving a Death

Regardless of our theological orientation or faith tradition, death has an impact like no other experience; it is the grandmother of all grief. "It's so final," is the mantra that grieving women wail around the world. The loss of a loved one into the arms of death allows for no other scenario but "gone." Indeed, nothing is ever the same when the void of death visits our hearts.

In all our experiences of loss, we are most challenged to grieve well when we are faced with the death of someone we love. The two most powerful guidelines to live by during this time are: *I will grieve with a passion* and *I will get through this*...and truly believing and living one is impossible without believing and living the other.

I Will Grieve With a Passion

Our culture is not "death friendly." It once was. In times past, the experience of dying took place in the home, and family members washed and dressed the body and hosted the wake.

We "do" death differently today. First, we arrange—often at great expense—extensive cosmetic delicacies around the practical details of death. Because we don't want to look death in the face—literally—we "make arrangements" that camouflage the reality of life leaving the body. Next, we allow ourselves to be distracted from our own needs to focus on "the way he (she) would have wanted it." We neglect the details of what is truly meaningful and symbolic to us in an attempt to meet the needs of our loved one—who actually has no need of our details. Finally, we get caught in the culture's harsh demand to "be strong," when, in reality, death brings us to our knees with pain, fear, and confusion. We are showered with the physical, emotional, and spiritual support of family and friends as we move through those first few weeks—only to find that with their departure, nothing strong remains, except a pain that *strong* comes nowhere near defining.

Grieving the death of a loved one takes passion, and women know passion; we are passionate creatures. Life to us is a tapestry of relationships of every color and texture—and when a loved one dies, our entire life tapestry is severely disrupted. We weave with passion; we grieve with passion.

The challenge to us through this journey, then, is to claim for ourselves that which we need—no small task. After all, most of us spend our lives defining our needs by determining the needs of others and doing what we can to participate in filling those needs. We are lovers; we are proud of this nurturing side of ourselves and seldom apologize for it—and we need not, especially when we grieve. English poet Maureen Duffy captures the force of love facing death in her poem "Wounds": "Love...is...the only effective counter to death." What's more, our desire to support the needs of others is consistent with all major religions: to live in love, with and for others.

So, when death grips life, we are caught in a dilemma. We are passionately aware of our own needs—yet equally attuned to the needs of others who are hurting with grief as well. Our natural and immediate response, often, is to move in the direction of touching the needs of others—and this is certainly part of what we need to do at this time. But to neglect our own needs right now is to diminish the full spectrum of the grief work we have to do. Our nature will drive us to care for others—while our pain presses in on our inner world, demanding to be touched and soothed as well. Our passion, when grieving well, will not let us deny or neglect that pain.

"When Hal died," Betty recalls, "my sister and

her husband stayed with me for several weeks. During that time, I wanted to go to the graveyard each day. There was something about just being there next to the fresh mound of dirt that brought Hal back just a little. I would stand there and sob, touch the soil, talk to Hal, and go back home. But I really hated asking my brother-in-law to drive me out there. I would apologize all the way out and all the way back, but I was doing what I knew I had to do during those first couple of weeks." Today, Betty makes no apologies. "If I hadn't gone every day, I would never have faced the reality of Hal's death as soon as I did. I just had to ask that my needs then and there be taken care of."

Perhaps one of our most passionate needs in grieving the death of a loved one is our need to cry. Once again, sensitive to the fact that our tears are going to make others uncomfortable, we often gulp, inhale, choke—anything to keep the tears from flowing. We'll even "hide out" to do our crying, for fear that our tears are somehow unworthy of public view. But why? Grief is pain—often physical pain. If we deserve anything during this time, we deserve the right to cry, bawl, wail. We are angry, confused, and frightened, and crying is a natural response to such brutal realities. To throw ourselves into our tears is to let the passion flow out into life, where it belongs. Studies on grief show that those who are not afraid of or embarrassed by their tears begin to find meaning in life—even joy—much more quickly than those who try to "be strong."

All This as a Woman

- *How do you express passion? How can your personal expression of passion be brought out in the grief you are currently experiencing?*
- *What are your needs right now—practical, emotional, and spiritual? Make a list and include as many details as possible. Name one way you can go about getting each of those needs met during this time.*
- *What is one of your fondest memories of your deceased loved one? Bring that memory to mind with lots of detail, and allow yourself to cry deeply with the memory.*

I Will Get Through This

In the grip of grief, this is the hardest fact to hear and believe. We hurt to the core of life—to such depth that it feels as if the pain is becoming a part of who we are. The fact is, the pain is exactly who we are in the midst of grief. We *are* human pain and there is absolutely no escape. There is only "getting through."

Oh how our hearts demand to know "How?" What is the formula? What is the remedy? What is the pain-killer? The loneliness, sadness, anger, and confusion are constant reminders that a precious part of life is gone, and we only want to know how we're supposed to live with this pain for the rest of our lives.

How? By claiming a belief in our inner strength—
"I will get through this." Without this belief, the journey is long and dark. Minute to minute, especially
when the pain is at its worst, we must hear our own
voices declare this out loud. We must say to ourselves and to the world: "I will get through this." We
must also hear this affirmation within the depths of
our being, where the pain is most at home. There,
where the darkest strands of grief are known only to
ourselves, we have to believe what French philoso-
pher and mystic Simone Weil tells us: "If we go
down into ourselves we find that we possess exactly
what we desire." Only then do we take the first step
toward "getting through." Only then do we tap our
deep pool of personal wisdom to find our way into
the very center of grief. Only then can we begin the
process of coming out on the other side.

One of the most significant factors in our ability
to go down into ourselves—where we can hear the
affirmation "I will get through this"—is the set of
details surrounding the death we grieve. For example, an expected death resulting from a lingering illness or a natural deterioration of the body due to age
affords us the gift of time. We are surrounded with a
sort of buffer zone between the dawn of reality—
death is imminent—and the loss itself. This can be a
dark and painful zone, no doubt about it, but that
zone of time gives us precious opportunities to
remember, to share tears with the loved one we will

soon lose, to make arrangements. "My twin brother and I spent a lot of time together in the last seven months of his life," Connie remembers. "We told childhood stories to each other that we'd never shared before, and we talked about what my life would be like without him. What I treasured most were those times when he asked me about how I was going to grieve. Those were really incredible moments. I would tell him what I thought I would probably do, and then, after he died, I did just what I said I'd do—and it was like he was right there with me because we'd talked about it. Life just got so precious to us during those months, and death lost most of its horrible threat."

Given time, we find ourselves open to those moments of intimacy when we're strong enough to be vulnerable. As a result, we can hear our inner wisdom: "I will get through this." We've had the blessed opportunity to live with death in a way that actually begins to bring about new life.

Not so with sudden—especially violent—death. When the day starts with its usual routine and ends with a devastating hole in it because a loved one suddenly dies, we have those added layers of shock that leave us numb and confused. We simply cannot hear "I will get through this" in those first weeks and months—in fact, we can hear nothing but the chambers of our soul wailing "Noooo!"

Once again, time is a crucial factor. While an

expected death *gives us time*, a sudden death forces us to *give ourselves time*, and, in our immediate-gratification society, few of us know how to do this. Trying to continue with routines while pouring massive amounts of energy into our pain, we actually *lose* time—or our familiar awareness of time. Either time slows to an eternity a minute or it passes through our days unnoticed, and thus lost.

Our grief work in the face of sudden death is to *give ourselves time* for reality to become real. Rather than listening to the voices that seem to insist we "get on with life," we wait, without self-expectations, for that first faint whisper: "I will get through this." We *will* hear it in the process of giving ourselves time.

All This as a Woman

- *How can you claim for yourself the affirmation, "I will get through this"? Does writing help? Does recording and listening to your own voice help?*
- *How did you "get through" other major disappointments and losses in life? Be specific about details. Will anything from those times help you now?*
- *Do you know a woman who has encountered tremendous grief? Can you talk with her about her own "getting through"?*
- *Are you comfortable sharing your grief with others? Will a support group of grieving women be beneficial to you?*

The Sacred Pieces

There is an ancient Indian tale of a young woman grieving the loss of her beloved. So deep was her pain that she was sure it would destroy her. A wise and passionate grandmother suggested that she visit local homes and continue to make visits until she found a woman who grieved more deeply than she did. The young woman did just that, and returned to the wise grandmother a week later. "My grief is lighter—for I have walked the way of grief with every other woman."

It takes time to find what will support our grief work—for what supports one woman may not be especially helpful to another. The young woman in the Indian story found listening to the grief of other women to be her way through. This is true for many women, but it isn't necessarily true for all of us. After all, we are unique in our individual personalities, and our personal situations are vastly different. Some of us will find support groups helpful; for others, talking one-on-one may by more helpful.

As we set out to find our way through—unique as each way will be—there are, however, a number of sacred pieces that we do share from the outset. Some of these pieces are the basic characteristics of grief; others are practical guidelines; others are directions for the soul. In one way or another, these sacred pieces are common to all of us, and knowing what they are will help us find those distinctive means we are looking for to "get through."

The sacred void: Whether our loss is sudden or the result of a lingering condition that meant inevitable death, our first reaction is disbelief. A brief minute ago, our loved one was "alive," occupying a place in our lives that we've defined day by day. Then, in a heartbeat, that person does not occupy that place anymore—not like before. We are numb; we feel hollow and confused. As the rush of "no" consumes all the air, we find it hard to breathe—as if death were sucking everything into itself. Many women have used words like *disoriented* and *confused* to describe this moment.

Following on the heels of this moment—sometimes within minutes—we begin to ask, "What do I do?" Our natural human strength opens wide the doors of practicality, and we begin a mental shopping list of what needs to be done: where we need to go, who needs to be phoned, what arrangements need to be made. This is a primary coping mechanism that serves us well in the moment of shock. The Creator knew the numbing power of grief and graciously packaged us with the blessing of practical details.

With time, the sacred void will press in on us in deeper ways. We will find ourselves trying to define who we are, now that this beloved person is no longer with us. A major measure of our pain has to do with the love we brought to the relationship. The love is still there. It doesn't die; it never will. But the usual channel for that love has changed into what feels like a void. The love exists—perhaps feeling stronger than ever—but our opportunities to deliver the love no longer exist.

An awareness of this missing channel of expressing and receiving love pulls us toward anger. Author Elisabeth Kubler-Ross names anger as one of the most critical aspects of our suffering the experience of grief. This anger is always about many things, but perhaps one of the most subtle yet respect-worthy dimensions of anger is our loss of specialness. As caring creatures, women are going to cringe at this reality, but think about it for a minute. Lillian puts it beautifully: "I knew Richard loved me more than anyone else in the world. I was special to him in so many ways that were all mine and I absolutely loved the way I delighted him. About two months after his death, I was crying and missing him so badly I just lashed out with, *Will I ever be that special to someone again?* At first, I just couldn't stay with that thought; it sounded so conceited. But I kept going back to it and in a few days I could admit that it was a fact: I was angry because I had lost the one person who thought I was absolutely wonderful."

This is appropriate, respectable anger—as is all the anger we experience in the midst of grief. Our work, when anger rushes in, is to call it what it is:

grief's sibling. It is normal; even in its intensity and self-centeredness, grief's anger deserves all respect.

With time, the rushes of anger will become fewer and less intense—and this is an important milestone. Our grief work is bearing fruit when we can look back over the week and see that our moments of anger are not so obvious. At this point, we will also bring to mind a few moments of peace, simple as they may be: a good night's sleep, laughter at someone's joke, the simple joy of seeing a squirrel outside the living-room window. This is when we will know we have walked all the way into and through a sacred void, and are beginning to feel the breeze of new life brushing our heart.

The sacred memories: As women, with all threads of life connected at some level to all other threads of life, we have a wonderfully inexhaustible capacity to store memories. When we are moving through grief, this can be both a curse and a blessing. Depending on what we do with our memories, we either move toward new beginnings or we get snagged on crippling sadness, guilt, remorse, and useless romanticism.

Our memories are going to press in on us with titanic strength in the first weeks and months following the death of a loved one. Every sense is going to remind us of something about the person: the smell of coffee in the morning, the toothbrush in the medicine cabinet, the phone bill, a song on the radio. Each tiny reminder takes us back to something we associated with the person who is no longer here: "He always fixed the coffee in the morning;" "What do I do with this toothbrush?" "Here's the bill for the call I made to him when he flew to Chicago to close that deal;" "We always sang together when that song came on."

Trying to avoid these memories is like trying not to breathe. We have to go back into the life we knew when our loved one was here. We have to see, hear, touch, taste, smell things that are going to heighten our savage awareness that this precious person is gone. If we're too hard on ourselves with these inescapable and inevitable details, we will suffocate with crippling sadness. With a passion, we have to say, "Yes, this reminds me—and yes, that reminds me, and yes, that too!" To deny these connections or to beat ourselves up because they hurt so bad is to sidestep a part of the suffering that we have to go through. We end up building a barrier of crippling sadness that makes our journey through grief very, very long.

When my father died, my youngest son, Thomas, could not attend the funeral with me; he doesn't live with me. (Talk about grief!) Several weeks after the funeral, when Thomas and I had a chance to visit, we sat down and went through the pictures I had taken of the military funeral my father had been given. The flag-draped casket ("Granddad's casket"), the 21-gun salute, the presentation of the crisply folded flag to my grieving mother ("Grandma"), and the casual pictures of the family gatherings throughout the week: I sobbed then and I weep now as I write. That was a time of remembering for me, and a time of deep grieving for Thomas. Naturally, as the weeks, months, and years unfolded, my memories and my grieving would broaden and deepen. But sharing the pictures and their accompanying story with Thomas was perhaps the first step I took along the route of grieving well.

More difficult than the daily reminders, however, are those memories that gave character to the relationship we shared with this person. These memories are going to range from happy to sad, from meaningful to mean. We will have years of these memories, some public and known to others, some private and known only to ourselves and our loved one. These are the memories that are sacred and will serve us well in getting through. These are the basic substance we use to do the real work of grieving the fact that nothing will ever be the same. And this is where we can get caught in guilt, remorse, and romanticism if we don't seize the opportunity to relate with our memories in healthy ways.

Just a few basic guidelines that help us use sacred memories to get through: First, and most important, we have to go get the memories. Sure, many will come unbidden, but the work of grief involves active, purposeful remembering. We don't wait for the memories to come to us at some unguarded moment. Rather, we actively decide to remember—and then go back in our relationship as far as we can remember.

We have to get the good memories and the bad memories—everything; and for once, we don't need to worry about detail or accuracy. We want to get the laughter and the tears, the beginnings and the endings, the highs and lows. We want to collect that which is public and get those precious secrets. We also want to feel all the emotions our memories arouse. We want to feel the joy and the sadness, the happiness and the regrets, the peacefulness and the anger. We want to remember those times when our relationship was damaged because of something one of us did or failed to do, and we want to remember those times when our relationship seemed strong as a rock and could hold solid through anything.

With this collection of sacred memories—and they're all sacred—we're able to keep a healthy perspective on reality. We won't get caught in guilt because we'll touch failure on both sides of the relationship. We won't get caught in remorse because we'll acknowledge the full breadth of every aspect of the relationship. We won't get caught in romanticism because we will actively remember how riddled with human nature the relationship actually was.

This is not a "do it some Saturday afternoon" pastime, or a "once and be done with it" exercise. Sacred memories are with us constantly, especially during our early weeks and months of severe grieving. Going and getting the memories is critical "filler" work, perfect for those driving, washing-dishes, scrubbing-the-tub times when other, usually negative, thoughts try to fill our minds. This may be one of the best things we do for ourselves in the journey through grief. Holding our memories sacred helps us see the promise in our future.

The sacred future: Facing, entering, and moving through the sacred void, and working with our sacred memories, leads to a sacred future. We begin to really believe, "I will get through this." More and more, we become aware of less weight on our heart, less darkness around the corners of life. We begin to take delight in simple things and find ourselves ready for some of the major decisions that have been awaiting our attention. Vera's son was killed in Viet Nam. "For seven months, I just couldn't focus on anything. I kept thinking about how wonderful Jake made me feel to be his mother. He'd send me things from overseas that told me how much he missed me. And then the memories—I kept remembering when he was born, his first birthday, his first day of school, the time he got suspended from school, his high-school graduation, the day he enlisted. I can see now that I missed being special, and that just going over and over those memories actually helped me get through. After seven months, I just got up one morning and went to the phone and called the newspaper to place a classified ad for his car that had been sitting in the garage all that time." Vera entered the sacred void, went and got her sacred memories, and stepped into a sacred future. She didn't exactly know what she was doing at the time, but in reflecting on that suffering, "the worst I've ever known," she admits, Vera got through. Today, she coordinates a grief center for parents whose children have died violently.

All This as a Woman

- *How did you first respond to the news that someone you love had died? Do words like* disoriented *and* confused *work for you? What other words are descriptive of that moment?*
- *What grocery list did you mentally put together immediately following the news of the death?*
- *What did your loved one do to make you feel special?*
- *What parts of your day lend themselves to sacred memories? Driving or commuting? Household chores? Bathing, walking, just before falling asleep?*
- *What might you do with the wisdom you are gaining from getting through this experience of grief? Do you have something special to offer others who are perhaps suffering severe grief and seem helpless to cope?*

All that we love deeply becomes a part of us.

HELEN KELLER

CHAPTER THREE

The Changing Face of Love: Grieving a Relationship

I have spent the last 15 minutes at the front door of our home, watching my 19-year-old son load boxes, bags, bookcases, lamps, stereo, and speakers into the back of his pickup truck. He just ran in, gave me a kiss on the cheek, and said, "I'll be back for another load in a few hours." Neumann is moving out. Although he's moving a mere 15-minute drive from here and planning for the move has been evolving over the last three months, it's still hard to see him go. I'm grieving.

My son isn't dying; he isn't moving halfway across country, like his brother did six months ago; and we aren't experiencing this move as "good riddance." But I can't deny the fact that I've been griev-

ing for several weeks as this date has drawn closer.
Tonight, when I turn out the lights and lock up, I'll
listen to the heartbeat of our home and know that it's
different: Neum doesn't live here anymore. I'll go to
bed wondering how he's doing, this "first night" on
his own. Oh, he'll be a phone call away, but I will
know some sharp grieving in those dark hours
before I drift off to sleep.

What am I grieving? What have I lost? A number
of things. For one thing, the rhythm of our household
will be different. The ebb and flow of our routine will
be unfamiliar for a while as we adjust to one less
human being to factor into meal planning, household
chores, leisure hours—and the orchestration needed
to accommodate all of us in the morning with just
one bathroom. (That will be an easy adjustment!) The
geography of the house may change since we now
have extra space. The very atmosphere will be different; Neumann was our stand-up comic. When family
issues became tense, Neum could find the humor
and bring us all to laughter with a simple observa-
tion of human nature.

Mostly, I grieve the changing relationship I share
with Neum. He's my son and always will be. But
"we" will be different. With my son's moving out,
we shift toward parent/adult-child relating. I've
been through this with Neum's two older brothers
and older sister, so I'm not a rookie. But each shift is
different because each relationship is unique and

each set of circumstances is different. In this rite of passage for Neum, I look forward to much that is new—but I also must do my grieving.

Love, Loss, and Self

Next to death, grief resulting from a changing relationship may be one of the most painful experiences we face. After all, women are first and foremost relational creatures. Our relationships are precious to us and define who and what we are in the world. We draw life from our relationships and put much of our own lives into nurturing them. When our primary relationships change, even for the better, we will grieve what was good and familiar before the change.

The greatest challenge to us in these situations is our sense of self. In relationship, we name ourselves: mother, lover, sister, daughter, friend. At a very deep level, we even name ourselves as a certain kind of mother, lover, sister, daughter, friend. "I am a good mother." "I am a passionate lover." "I am a sensitive sister." "I am a reliable daughter." "I am a supportive friend." When the relationship changes, for whatever reason, our self-identity changes as well. Lisa recalls part of the grief she experienced when her neighbor and good friend moved 300 miles away: "Jenny called one night to say that her 'new' neighbors helped her and her husband unload some of the heavier furniture into their 'new' apartment. When I got off the phone, I started crying as I pictured Jenny's new friends. I was jealous. I was no longer someone she could turn to for a simple helping hand." Lisa and Jenny would remain intimate friends despite the miles, but the little pieces of friendship they had shared for years were gone. No more chats across the back fence, no more shared yard sales, no more borrowing household items. These things, so little and seemingly insignificant, are part of the mortar of a friendship, and for Lisa and Jenny, these were gone. Both women had to re-identify themselves in relationship to the other.

Much like naming our grief, re-naming our selves is contingent upon so many variables. Perhaps the two most critical details in re-naming ourselves in the changing face of love are the nature of the relationship itself and the kind of change that is taking place.

Recall, for example, my son's moving out. Neum and I share a wonderful mother/son relationship. We've been through some tough times, especially when his father and I divorced, but we've never felt our relationship was seriously damaged. We've had the usual parent/child tensions, disagreements, and disappointments, but we share a great deal of common respect, trust, and love. Nothing in our joint history has left us damaged in a major way. The nature of our relationship is very good.

What's more, the kind of change our relationship

will experience as a result of his moving out is a common occurrence for all parent/adult-child relationships. It's a healthy, inevitable shift that every mother must eventually embrace and support. It's a grief that women are willing to name, to talk about, to deal with.

If I needed support in this experience, I have a lot going for me. First, I have very little guilt relative to my role as mother to Neum. Oh sure, every mother feels that she could have done better by her child, and I have some of that. But Neum and I are "good," as the kids say these days. Second, I have the respect of family and culture in this experience. Plenty of other women have known this experience and could help me find my own way through the normal grief of a mother watching her child grow up—and away. My grief is acceptable, and re-naming my identity will be a process that women have experienced and shared since the beginning of time.

But what if the history of my relationship with Neum were scarred? What if we had major issues of abuse, distrust, abandonment, neglect? What if Neum's moving out were an act of escape on his part—or worse yet, throwing him out on my part? My experience of grief would be altogether different from what I'm knowing now. My pain would be different—and probably a great deal sharper. Re-naming my identity would be a long process that would involve guilt and forgiveness and healing. I would

still, however, have my family's and society's acceptance of what I was going through: a mother grieving
the changing relationship with her son.

Not all changing relationships receive such support and acceptance, however. I think of Karen, a
married woman and mother of three who fell in love
with another man. Karen and I have spent countless
hours talking about her feelings for this person, a co-
worker, and have often found some consolation in
naming her feelings as "just infatuation." But Karen's
feelings are real and deep. She has never had an
affair with this man, but she cares for him deeply in
a way that is not acceptable to her family or society.
Karen has never even expressed her personal feelings
to this man; he knows nothing of her affections.

Now, the man is leaving the company for another
position and Karen is faced with grieving and re-
naming her sense of identity, much as I am dealing
with my son's moving out. But unlike my grief,
Karen's grief and changing identity will have little
support. She doesn't feel free to speak of her grief,
and she won't find much reading material that will
respectfully address her needs as a grieving woman.
By cultural standards, her grief is illegitimate. In fact,
she may even have a hard time respecting herself
because of the norms of acceptability that her reli-
gion, family, and culture have named for her. For
Karen, the changing face of love will be a dark and
lonely experience.

All This as a Woman

- *What relationship in your life is in the process of change? Is this a "socially acceptable" relationship?*

- *What words come to mind as you look back on this relationship and identify yourself in it? Try words like* good, passionate, sensitive, reliable, supportive.

- *Are you generally satisfied with what this relationship has been like in the past? Do you wish certain major aspects of the relationship had been different? Is this contributing to your grief?*

- *What day-to-day details of your life are going to be different as a result of the loss you are experiencing in this relationship? Can you anticipate these changes in a way that will minimize the pain—such as avoiding certain places and activities, at least for a while?*

The Myth of Letting Go

We do not deal with the changing face of love by letting go; that's a myth. The simple fact is, we never let go. This relationship has been a part of our lives in some way, for some period of time, and it will be present to us for the rest of our lives. It held meaning for us; it held definition. It became part of the fabric of our lives and had a character all its own—almost like a personality. It was lively, joyful, exciting; it was oppressive, fearful, dreary. It brought life; it brought death. It contributed to rounding out life for us; it diminished life for us. Whatever it was, it was a relationship that is now different, and we grieve that change. The person we are today, facing the changes

in the relationship, is not the person who entered
that relationship or journeyed through that relationship. And we will not be the same person tomorrow,
looking back on today and yesterday. The fact
remains: we simply do not let go. What we do is
open our arms and cease to cling. That's the direction
we want to go—we have to go.

I remember catching fireflies as a child. They
were a delight to watch, as their momentary blip of
light pierced the nearing darkness and then van-
ished. I didn't even really know where they were
until they lit up, but as soon as I saw that flash, I
pursued and captured. As soon as I caught one,
though, something inside me became very uncomfortable, as if I were engaged in an unnatural act. It
didn't feel right to hold that small creature cupped in
my hands, or to drop it in the nearby jar. Invariably,
I'd sweep my arms up over my head, open my
hands, and let the firefly return to its nocturnal dance
whenever it was ready to take flight. I'd then settle
for the satisfaction of just watching the light show.

Relationships are like that. They come into our
lives as light, often piercing an inner darkness we're
not even aware of. Like a child drawn to the firefly's
point of light in the dusk, we are drawn into relationship with the light of hope. We don't exactly capture
the relationship, but we invest that part of ourselves
that gives birth to hope and promise. When the relationship changes, for whatever reason, it is as unnat-

ural for us to cling to the old as it was for me to cling to my captured firefly. Some, if not all, of the hope we brought into the relationship fades or changes, and we have to throw open our arms, heavy with grief, to allow the change. We don't let go; we simply cease to cling to the same kind of hope we once had.

Our ceasing to cling, however, is supported by our self-identity and love of self. Recall that grieving is a self-centered experience. In the changing face of love, we grieve by first naming ourselves and caring enough for ourselves to cease clinging. As Neum moves into adulthood, I am no less his mother; he is no less my child. Nothing will ever change the fact that we are parent and child, so I am not threatened by the change we're going through. Rather, the process of self-identification for me involves my basic definition of *mother*. For me, that expands to include a healthy dose of friendship as my kids get older. I remember the first "legal" alcoholic drink I shared with my son Jerome. I had such a good time going into a bar and buying us drinks. In that small window of time, we were more like a couple of long-time friends, kicking back to catch up on the small details of life.

That's our challenge when a relationship changes. If we can make our prayer, "I shall not cling," we can see a broader horizon of possibilities. We can see more clearly that we *were* one thing and now we *are* something else. Recall Jenny and Lisa, the women whose friendship was challenged as a result of Jenny's relocation. They have simply redefined how they experience themselves, individually and together, given their new circumstances. They've accomplished this in a number of ways, one being weekly phone visits. They've set aside every Wednesday evening, 9:30 P.M.-10:00 P.M., as their time to visit. They don't always have big news to share or need major emotional support. In fact, most of the time they simply share the week's activities with each other, much as they would if they chatted across the back fence. Should they need more from each other, the little things of life are in place to make them always available. Jenny and Lisa are as intimate as ever—only in a different way.

All This as a Woman

- *What hope did you bring into the relationship you are currently grieving?*
- *What do you miss about the relationship? Note as many details as possible. What do you miss most? What will you miss least?*
- *Can you express what you are grieving to another person? If not, can you express it in some way for yourself, such as writing or talking out loud as if you were talking to the other person?*
- *If this loss in the relationship had not happened, what might the relationship have been like a year from now? Since this loss has happened, what do you see yourself being like a year from now?*

Braving Bitterness

As I listen to women tell their stories of loss and grief in relationship, I hear a recurring pattern. Women who avoid becoming bitter, or allow themselves only a brief time of bitterness, seem to grieve in healthier ways than those who let bitterness become part of their re-identification process.

Bitterness is the souring of the soul. It's that dark veil that coats life and leaves even our sweetest joys laced with insufficiency. Although being bitter is a human reaction—and not at all uncommon in the experience of grief—it holds the lethal potential of poisoning life.

Barbara could have been bitter. When she and her former husband divorced three years ago, the court awarded primary custody of their two minor children to the children's father. She has regular visitation with her children, but "it's not the same," Barbara says. "I don't get to be there in the middle of the night with them when they need someone; I don't get to see them off to school in the morning; I don't get to kiss their 'ouchies.'" Barbara was angry at the court's decision, but she hasn't let that anger turn her bitter. "If I got bitter, my kids would only suffer more—and I would too. I've just tried to be a mother to the kids in new ways. I'm not the custodial parent, but I'm not an absent parent either. I love every minute I'm with my kids, and I don't look at it as 'that's all I get.' Rather, I look at it as 'this is it' and

I just get in there and enjoy the kids. I don't feel like something's been taken away from me."

How do we know if we're bitter—or are becoming that way? We simply ask ourselves, "Where is my energy going? When I feel angry about the loss or change in this relationship, do I focus on circumstances and other persons, or do I focus on myself?" After all, being bitter takes time and energy from self re-naming and gives it to areas over which we have no control. It focuses on outside circumstances or other persons, and leaves us too fatigued to use the fine building blocks we have to re-name ourselves in the relationship. Barbara puts it beautifully: "I don't feel like I'm 'making do.' That would make me the victim or the loser. Instead, I am a winner of a mother—I just know that." Barbara didn't begin to work with what she's got; she started with 100 percent of everything she is.

All This as a Woman
- *When have you experienced bitterness in the past?*
- *As you think about the relationship you are grieving, what are the specific changes or losses that make you angry? Is this anger turning to bitterness?*
- *Where is the focus of your energy as you grieve this relationship? When you look in the mirror, do you see just yourself, or do you see yourself in relationship?*
- *What are your strongest qualities as a person? How can you use these qualities to re-name yourself as you grieve?*

When we grieve,
we grieve the loss
of what something
meant to us,
not the object itself.

JOAN GUNTZELMAN

CHAPTER FOUR

The House that Life Built: Grieving a Possession

Not all major grief is experienced as a result of a loved one dying or a significant relationship changing. In her classic work, *Necessary Losses: The Loves, Illusions, Dependencies and Impossible Expectations That All of Us Have to Give Up in Order to Grow*, author Judith Viorst sums up the breadth of these countless and profound losses: "Our losses include not only our separations and departures from those we love, but our conscious and unconscious losses of romantic dreams, impossible expectations, illusions of freedom and power, illusions of safety—and the loss of our own younger self, the self that thought it would always be unwrinkled and invulnerable and immortal."

These losses have to do with "the rest of life"—those other parts of ourselves that contribute to our sense of identity, comfort, security, pleasure. The following list of losses is hardly exhaustive, and you are encouraged to add to it, especially as you read this chapter: job loss, relocation, mastectomy, destroyed home, aging, the loss of privacy, independence, space, financial security, dreams, beliefs, faith, a treasured object, personal image, personal recognition.

Embrace Attachment

Some words in the language of our culture have simply gotten a bad name for themselves. *Attachment* is one of those words. How often we hear that being attached to something is somehow a flaw in our moral character! If we're attached to our car, our home, our lovely yard, our collection of figurines, a comfortable pair of shoes or old housecoat, we often find ourselves somewhat embarrassed and perhaps even the victim of playful but nonetheless hurtful teasing. Attachment automatically implies that we're immature, childish, selfish, lacking a sense of what's really valuable in life.

Too bad, for the fact is, women experience attachment as a way of relating with the world. We embrace attachment; we actually rely on attachments to help us create life structures such as our sense of self, our sense of life's continuity, our sense of groundedness. We're not afraid to be attached to something because, as relational creatures, attachment comes naturally to us. In fact, we probably don't give much thought, on a day-to-day basis, to being attached to that which is important to us. I often pull out the "good china," for example, to use on special occasions—and sometimes to make non-special occasions special. Grandma Bess gave me that set of china over 25 years ago, and yes, when I think about it, I'm attached to it. I'm proud of it; it holds special meaning for me because Grandma gave it to me; it's lovely to handle and look at.

In woman-language, attachment has little to do with practical or market value. That's one of the reasons women are accused of being "irrational creatures." We have an inner system that holds precious an entire universe of treasures, a system that we seldom defend or even define. Yet, when we cry or get angry over the broken vase, we often face criticism for what is labeled "emotional behavior." In actuality, we're grieving.

Each of us could probably list, in a very short period of time, at least a dozen things to which we're attached. We may feel a little silly about our attachments, and we may not be able to articulate exactly why we're attached to them. But we know deep within—where our love of life resides—that we do, indeed, treasure these objects and are attached to them.

Naturally, our degree of attachment ranges from mild to major. I would associate mild attachment, for example, with Grandma's china, Mother's old rocker, and my kids' baby pictures. I would associate major attachment to my wedding band, my home, my health. The loss of any of these, regardless of where they fall on my attachment spectrum, would bring me grief. Naturally, I will grieve more deeply over the loss of something to which I have a major attachment.

All This as a Woman

- *Make a list of what you are attached to and then align your treasures along an "attachment spectrum." Cluster your mild attachments toward the left end of the spectrum and cluster your major attachments toward the right end of the spectrum. You might even want to be very specific, with detailed increments along your spectrum.*
- *Where would you position any loss you are currently experiencing? Does your loss fall toward the mild-attachments end of the spectrum or the major-attachments end?*

Carving Out Our Own Respect

Carving out is an apt metaphor indeed. Imagine for a moment the careful attention given to the selection of a grave stone and the engraving that it will bear for centuries. The name must be exact—no misspellings are tolerated on a tombstone. Birth and death dates are accurate and positioned in a balanced fashion. We often select a fitting inscription or symbolic image to warm the otherwise cold and final statement that a loved one passed this way.

Such care and precision, however, are seldom given to so many of the other major losses we experience. In fact, we don't even relate grief to the experience. Oh, we may say that Mary "lost her home in the flood," Vicky is "losing her youthful vitality," or Norma "lost her faith." But from there, we rush to the emotions of sadness, anger, or confusion—all natural and acceptable emotions—especially if we are Mary, Vicky, or Norma. But we don't give sufficient acknowledgment to the reality that these emotions are, in fact, major characteristics of grief.

Why don't we grieve these losses with greater respect, greater passion? The answer is twofold. First, our culture doesn't respect these losses the way it respects death and relationship changes. When we check the shelves at our favorite bookstore, for example, we can note the vast selection of titles that will support us in grieving a death or our pain in relationship. But we won't find a single title on grieving when our home has been destroyed or when the neighbor's dog has torn up our prized rose garden. We'll probably find titles on job loss or the trauma of having a mastectomy, but seldom will these titles focus primarily on the genuine and respectable grief involved in these experiences.

Second—and as a result of the fact that our culture doesn't respect these losses—we don't give ourselves permission to grieve. With hearts full of emotion, we go about tending to the practical details involved and neglect the real demands of grief. Somehow we think that "taking care of things" will alleviate—or at least discipline—our emotions so we can "get over it." In fact, we end up neglecting our desperate need to grieve.

Our work, then, is to carve out respect for the loss we experience and to give ourselves permission to grieve. Our emotions serve us well in this process.

We begin by respecting attachment. After all, we will never respect our loss and grieve with integrity if we don't respect the initial attachment. A note of clarity here: *respecting attachment* focuses on the way we feel (our emotions) toward a treasured object, and not on the object itself. Once again, we do not place value on a thing by some external set of standards; how we feel towards something needs absolutely no rationale whatsoever—and that's the respect we bring to attachment. We *just are attached,* and to respect our loss and give ourselves permission to grieve, we make no apologies for the attachment in the first place.

Next, we turn off the critical voices—including our own—that try to underplay the situation. We know our sadness and anger; we know we hurt. These emotions are ours, and to respect them we let no one judge them. We handle them as gently as we would the beloved treasure we have lost. We trust our feelings as a form of validation for our loss and grief. "When our home was burglarized," Paula remembers, "I was outraged and I wasn't afraid or ashamed of that. I didn't care if the police and news reporters wanted their version of 'just the facts.' I didn't care if they thought I was somehow at fault because I lived in 'this neighborhood,' as they put it, and didn't have an alarm system for my house and car. What belonged to me had been criminally taken from me, and I wanted them to know all the facts about that—and my rage was one of them." Paula respected her loss; she allowed no one to be critical by imposing another version of the situation on her emotions.

At some point in the process of carving out our own respect, we must take up the challenge of being brutally honest with reality, and this involves avoiding inappropriate self-blame and accepting only the responsible fault that is legitimately ours to take. Because this venture relies on the passion of our emotions to pursue the objective facts, we do well to consider the input of a trusted friend. We want to take our emotions with us as we step back for a full-hearted view of what we have lost, and how—if at all—our own actions contributed to the loss. On the one hand, to carry inappropriate self-blame is to retard healthy grieving; we're burdened with a wall of regret and self-hostility that will not let us grieve fully and freely. On the other hand, to ignore legitimate responsibility is to enter denial where we risk inappropriate expressions of our precious emotions.

All This as a Woman

- *Are you comfortable with the fact that being attached to something is acceptable?*
- *Remember an emotional loss from childhood (not related to death or relationships). Were you able to express your emotions? Did anyone else understand your emotions? Can you respect the fact that you were simply and acceptably attached to that which you lost?*
- *Can you say to yourself, "I have a right to my feelings of anger and loss; my feelings are not right or wrong"? Why or why not?*
- *When you focus on your current loss, can you be objective about inappropriate self-blame and responsible fault that is legitimately yours to take? Who can you trust to help you with this?*

The Sacred Security Blanket

Judith Viorst launches her compassionate treatment of attachment, detachment, and grief with a careful review of the development of a child from birth to individuation. Simply bring to mind a small child clinging to what we usually refer to as a security blanket. This child has attached to the blanket as a point of security in the very natural process of detaching from Mother. In developmental psychology, the blanket is called a transitional object. With time, the child will feel sufficient internal security to detach from the blanket as well, moving toward a healthy individuated space.

When we lose something we've been attached to, part of our grieving will take us in the direction of a security blanket. This is as natural in the grieving process as is the child's need to cling to a transitional object. We grieve well when we recognize our security blankets for what they are: self-loving tools that support our journey.

Anna came home from the hospital feeling deformed and ugly after her mastectomy. She had been proud of her shapely figure and grieved deeply the loss of her "natural beauty," as she put it. "Before I returned to work, I started buying make-up and playing with different shades of mascara, eye shadow, lipstick, blush—the whole facial-beauty thing. I even went to one of the pricey department stores and got some professional consultation on color and brands. My first day back at work, I sported a face for the future. I felt pretty, feminine. My face gave me a sense of beauty that I felt I had lost when I lost my breasts." Anna continues with a sheepish grin: "Six months later, I couldn't be bothered with the make-up. It just didn't mean that much to me. It's as if I needed something to help me feel attractive for awhile, until I felt myself again."

Anna's story is deeply moving. It reaches into the core of every woman's life. After all, our breasts play a major role in our physical development as a girl-becoming-woman, in our ability to provide natural nourishment for a child, in the formation of our per-

sonal style of dress and fashion, and in our sexual
pleasures. Anna lost that part of herself and strug-
gled to find a new place of comfort within her body.
Paying careful attention to her face and experiment-
ing with a look that made her feel attractive served
as Anna's "security blanket" or "transitional object"
until she moved through grieving the loss of her
breasts. Time was her good friend.

For many of us, the very memory of our lost treasure will serve as our security blanket. Some of us, in
fact, may spend a lifetime carrying our security blanket with us in the form of searching for our lost treasure. This sacred search is natural, and we need to
allow ourselves the ongoing hope that searching
brings. Five years ago, for example, my son Jerome
gave me a beautiful set of prayer beads for Mother's
Day. I treasured those beads because they came from
my son as a statement of respect for my spirituality. I
could not handle those beads in prayer without
Jerome coming gently into my spirit. I carried them
in my coat pocket, in the bottom of my purse, in the
pockets of my slacks or work skirts; I was seldom far
from my beads. They served to focus my mind in
prayer and peace in the midst of rush-hour traffic, in
long waits for the doctor, in early-morning and late-
night times of worry.

I lost my prayer beads two years ago—and not a
week has gone by that I haven't hunted for them
somewhere. Sometimes I fall asleep at night trying to

think of where I haven't looked. Compulsing? Some may consider it that. I know, though, that I simply grieve the loss of a small part of myself, something that gave meaning and depth to my prayer, which brought meaning and depth to life. As long as my daily routines take me to places where I have prayed the beads, I will hold a small, shining piece of hope deep in my heart that I will find my beads. And believe me, if I do, the cosmos will celebrate!

I recall Belle's peaceful smile as she remembered her recent trip to the site of a home she once loved. "Exactly one year after the fire, I drove back to the vacant lot where our home had once stood. I sat there in the weeds and just 'listened' to the years of life that had happened in that now empty place. I cried, but the tears were cleansing. The home I had filled with love for my husband and my children was gone—but the love I had for them was as strong as ever." The vacant lot is now crowded with another home, a fenced-in yard, and a wide, paved driveway, but Belle drives by the site every year, on the anniversary of the fire, and remembers again that "there I once called home." Her security blanket—the location of her former home and the memories of that home—is her way of loving herself as she continues to grieve the loss of a great treasure.

All This as a Woman

- How comfortable are you with the thought of needing a sacred security blanket while you grieve your loss? Can you respect your need?
- What is serving you well as a security blanket in your grief? Do you have more than one security blanket? What has served you well as a security blanket in the past?
- Do you need your security blanket more at certain times of the day or during certain seasons of the year?
- Have you noticed that time is serving to be a good friend as you need your sacred security blanket less and less?

PART III

Grieving:
A How-to Manual

*Light tomorrow
with today.*

ELIZABETH BARRETT BROWNING

CHAPTER FIVE

A Wealth of Practical Strength

Certain characteristics of loss and grief are common to every human being. First, of course, is the very fact of grief: to be human is to grieve. Next, we all experience grief at an early age and on a regular basis. We don't grieve once, and then—having paid our dues and earned our stripes, so to speak—become exempt from future grief for the rest of our days. We grieve, in some way, every day of our lives.

We also face every possible degree of grief along a spectrum from mild to major. At times, our grief is subtle, gentle, and passing; at other times, our grief is so potent that it has the power to control the least significant dimensions of life, and seems to linger endlessly.

The final common ground that we all share in our grief is the fact that we all grieve *differently*.

Your Practical Grief Work

Your grief is uniquely yours, although there may be many details surrounding your current situation that are similar to what others are experiencing right now or have experienced in the past. Those similar details can prove to be channels for you to draw on as you find your way through the days, weeks, and months ahead. But ultimately, in the quiet recesses of your inner world, the journey through this grief is going to be yours; you are a solitary pilgrim. Now the good news—you are your own best guide, and you are capable of the task.

How long you grieve, how demonstrative you are with your grief, how you share your grief with others, and how your grief fits into your life structures and decisions: these parts of this grief belong solely to you. No one else can answer your questions about these practical "how-tos." No one can tell you that you should be crying more, that you should join a bereavement support group, that you should be getting on with your life. These are your determinations to make, and you will make them based on your own life history.

The following suggestions focus on practical measures that have helped women grieve every kind of loss. For your support, a small amount of detail is given to each suggestion—but these are *just suggestions*. There may be something here that resonates with a part of your life history, giving you a starting point from which to experiment with your own ways of practically coping with your grief.

Avoid major decisions: Grief is a shadowy experience. Because you are so acutely aware of your pain, you may not be aware of your attempts to grasp at relief. This shadowy side of grief makes you especially vulnerable, prone to certain "feels good" or "looks good" options. You may find yourself wanting to reach out at experiences and relationships that seem to hold the promise of relief—or at least temporary distraction—and you won't even be aware of what's going on. You'll make no connection between your grief and the options you're considering.

Some women, for example, find themselves making a major move, entering a new and intense relationship, venturing into a different career, only to find themselves a few months or a few years later deeply regretting their choices—and without making a connection between their choices and the grief they were experiencing. They simply do not see how their choices were connected to their desperate desire for relief.

Be alert to these kinds of significant, new-life directions. There will be a time for them at some point. For the time being, be willing to stay with the pain, for it will pass. Like ocean waves breaking in on the shore and flowing back out again into the sea, grief will dash up against your heart and then flush back. When the waves of grief are strong, all your energy is drawn into the moment, where it belongs. Don't rob that moment of your best attention by displacing your emotional energy with attempts to think. That time will come.

Tell your stories: Storytelling is as old as the human being. Long before civilizations were structured, people were telling their stories around campfires and on cave walls. Stories are the human tools that capture history and give what *was* to what *is*. As your memories cluster, you remember; as you remember, tell your stories—to yourself or to others. You may want to record your stories on tape, write them down, or ask a good friend to simply relax and let you reminisce. Don't worry whether your details of time and specific dialogue are accurate; you are not documenting history. Don't worry about choosing "good" stories instead of "bad" stories; you are not trying to entertain. Rather, you are healing through the ancient art of storytelling. You are keeping alive a part of you that simply cannot die: your love for what you have lost. Your stories help name and rename—thus memorializing—the respectful worth you place in what you have lost.

Be open to humor: Smiling, chuckling, and laughing are not disrespectful of grief. In fact, deep loss inevitably opens itself to laughter. Think for a

moment of the wakes and family gatherings after
funerals that you've attended. No doubt, laughter
was present as well as tears. Smiling and laughing
have direct effects on the body, relaxing muscles and
opening major arteries for healthier circulation.
Humor is God's way of moving us toward the light
in the midst of grief's darkness. Be willing to actively
pursue that which will make you laugh: television
programs, reading material, movies. Seek out enter-
tainment, family, and friends who will lighten your
spirit with the spice of laughter.

I recall the tears I shed as I watched my son
Joseph come down the aisle on his college graduation day, swaying to the familiar beat of "Pomp and
Circumstance." My "little boy," now all grown up,
was heading for all the risks of life. Then, as Joseph
glided into his seat in front of the stage, I saw the
message taped to the top of his mortarboard: "Why
me?" I didn't then—and I still don't—know what
Joseph was trying to say with that, but it struck me
as hilarious. My tears of grief turned into tears of
laughter.

Write letters: In his fantasy work *St. George and the
Dragon*, Edward Hays tells a story of how God decided to come to earth as ink, so as to be able to speak
to all people, in every language and culture. The
process of hand-holding-pen; releasing words as they
come, unedited; ink flowing as it will; brings out

your inner world. Writing is cleansing and renewing. Holding a friendly pen and writing on texture-friendly paper has a way of penetrating inner barriers to let out "stuff" we may not even be aware is "in there." Express yourself to a person—including yourself—or a thing. Open with affection ("Dear Me,") anger ("Damn you, Henry,") intensity ("Beloved Home,") or any other kind of greeting that comes naturally to you. Go on to express all your most intense emotions and deepest desires: be angry, silly, demanding. Write about the past, write about the future. Write about what never happened that you wish had, what happened that you wish hadn't, what happened that thrilled you.

Most of all, be honest. Don't edit your writing for grammatical correctness, content, or cohesiveness. It need have no polish to it whatsoever. The very activity of writing from the deepest parts of your emotions and memories is cleansing and healing. If you're not familiar with this kind of activity, experiment with short notes, postcard kinds of messages, and progress from there to longer missives. Consider saving what you write for future reading, or feel free to destroy it immediately. What you do with your end product is immaterial; the writing is what's important.

Change gradually: Nothing will ever be the same; that's the nature of loss. What you loved and were familiar with is not part of your life anymore. While facing the reality of "nothing ever being the same," go on to claim the rest of that reality: "things are different." With time, *very* different will be *somewhat* different—and with a little more time, *somewhat* different will become fully *familiar and normal.*

To move in that direction, be open to small measures of change—with the focus on *small.* Don't force new routines too quickly; don't consider major life changes. You are especially vulnerable right now, and while the pain may be obvious, your attempts to escape the pain may not be. While you manage with some things that absolutely have to be different as a result of your loss, hang on to some of the simple things you've done automatically for years. You may want to re-arrange the furniture, but don't make plans to relocate in the near future. You may want to take a class in twentieth-century literature, but don't launch into a four-year academic program. Change gradually by using what is familiar to build what is new. Your loss may mean major changes for you at some point, but not in the near future.

Befriend inactivity: As a woman, you are very much in touch with your body. As a grieving woman, however, you are at risk of letting your emotions overpower your body's voice. You are pouring out volumes of emotion and energy that you may not have even known existed in those deep and quiet parts of yourself. This is new territory for you, so to speak. As they say today, you've never been here before.

Be willing to nap, if you need to. Get comfortable with just sitting still and staring at the wall or petting the cat. Allow your body to check out of a world that demands productivity. Don't feel like everything you do must be obviously worthwhile. Your entire being is heavy with the work of grief right now. You know that through the experience of your mind and heart. You may not, however, know what stress your grief is putting on your body. Give it a chance to speak to you. Experiment with 60 seconds at a time. Sit down in a comfortable chair, gently lay your hands in your lap in a natural manner, breathe steadily, and remain still—for just one minute. Concentrate on only the passing of time. After about a minute, resume your usual activity. Enter inactivity several times a day and listen to your body as it begins to ask for longer and longer periods of stillness. Respect your body's request; give it the gift of stillness so it can regenerate itself. A lot of good can come from doing nothing!

Simplify: Procrastination often is considered a fault. Our culture judges procrastination as laziness, and religious traditions label it *sloth*. In reality, procrastination is neither laziness nor sloth, especially along the journey of grief. In the midst of grief work, procrastination can be our spirit's way of helping us simplify; it keeps us from becoming overwhelmed with details that, in the moment, are not especially relevant.

By resting in procrastination, you can put off doing today what can wait until tomorrow or until your natural energies allow you to focus. The rug does not have to be vacuumed today; balancing the checkbook can wait; you'll get around to sending out thank-you notes. When you throw yourself into these activities before your energies allow, you plant the early seeds of resentment. One woman even noted that she has never been able to wash the windows in spring and fall with the same gusto, pleasure, and satisfaction as she once brought to that chore because she forced herself to do it the spring her daughter died. Each season, when she sets out to wash the windows, she is overcome with the weight of the work, the mess, the time—and she knows she's connecting to the energy she misplaced that long-ago spring.

There are practical ways to simplify life during this time when energy is a scarce commodity. Consider, for example, arranging a "Things To Do" list into three categories, using an objective scale of "Must Do Today," "Can Do Tomorrow," and "Can Wait." Use your list as a discipline to prioritize—but use it as an affirmation as well. Add to your list as you need to, but also check off the things you do, as you would check off the items on your grocery list at the supermarket. Enjoy the sense of accomplishment you experience as you see the list grow shorter—and use the extra energy to grieve.

Note progress: Watch for your own milestones of progress: a brief burst of laughter or a passing smile, a sense of accomplishment with the completion of a few minor chores, a good night's sleep. These simple moments will tell you that the resources of practical strength you've been drawing on are, indeed, making you stronger. You are grieving well.

REMEMBER: There is no wrong way or right way to do the grief work you have to do.

All This as a Woman

- What are some of the changes you are considering right now—even if you're not giving a lot of serious thought to actually doing anything? Can you see a connection between these options and a search for relief from the pain of grief?

- When have you found yourself inspired and entertained by a story? What were the circumstances of that story? Was someone else telling you the story? Did you read it in a book? Did you hear it on the radio? Can you imagine yourself telling an inspiring or entertaining story that draws on your experience of grief?

- What experience do you have with sitting still? Were you forced to "sit in a corner" as a child? Will your past experiences leave you restless, perhaps feeling guilty, when you attempt to move into inactivity, even for a short period of time?

- What is your work ethic? Are you driven by a sense of worth based only on what you accomplish? How will your work ethic influence your attempts to simplify?

*If having
experiences is our
ordinary world,
what is the other
world, the other
fork in the road?*

CHARLOTTE JOKO BECK

CHAPTER SIX

A Wealth of
Spiritual Strength

Just as our life experience comes to bear on how we handle practical matters as we journey through grief, so too does it influence how we rely on our spiritual resources during this time. Many of us, for example, were raised within a specific religious tradition that shaped our values and morals—and even contributed to our weekly routines. We went to church on a weekly basis, received structured Sunday school lessons, and heard "God language" within the ebb and flow of our family life. Those who attended private, religious schools received this kind of formation on a daily basis.

Others of us may not have had a formal religious background. Even so, the human spirit is fashioned in the ways of the heart on a day-to-day basis by the atmosphere of love, peace, and respect that can be fostered within a family.

For some of us, our childhoods are burdened with shame, fear, and insecurity. But many of us can look back on our childhood with memories of being nurtured in ways that supported our personhood with an awareness of the divine and a sense of a benevolent Higher Power.

Your Spiritual Grief Work

Early life experiences are going to have a heavy impact on how we grieve as spiritual beings. When we enter the pain and darkness of grief, we are faced with the primordial questions, "What's it all about? What does this mean? Why did this happen? What now?" How we face these questions—not how we *answer* them, but how we *face* them—is shaped, to a large degree, by the way we've been introduced to realities beyond our sense awareness. How we face loss, perhaps life's greatest mystery, is shaped by how deeply we've ventured into the life of the spirit.

The following suggestions—and they are only *suggestions*—draw on the strength of your creative and intuitive nature. They tap into that part of you that goes beyond the "facts" of your life, that part that has been "self-shaped" within a world that is actually larger than life. For your support, a small amount of detail is given to each suggestion. There may be something here that resonates with a quiet but distantly familiar part of you, giving you a starting point from which to experiment with your own ways of spiritually coping with your grief.

Encourage yourself: The most important advice you will hear as you grieve will come from the wisdom of your own inner voice. This voice creates a constant chatter in your mind, and for the most part, you won't be aware of it. But it's there; just listen for it. You can hear it clearly during those "automatic pilot" times when you're engaged in routine, non-thinking activities like driving, doing household chores, enduring commercials in the middle of a television program. These are times when, with a little focus, you can see your mind jumping into worry, anger, fantasy, plans, memories. For example, one of the things my mind heads into—and I'm often not aware of it for minutes at a time—is a conversation I'm going to have with someone in the near future.

Focus on that inner voice during those times, and listen for any negative self-talk that drowns out your vast wealth of wisdom. When you hear that whining voice say, "This is awful. I'm never going to cope. I'm never going to be at peace again. Life holds so little for me from now on," be gentle with yourself. Talk back to the voice with that part of yourself that is wise and strong: "No, that's not correct. I am grieving. I did not ask for this grief, but it is here. I want to grieve well so that the person I will be on the other side of this grief will be whole and grounded. I am capable of grieving well. I will grieve well. The fact that I'm having this conversation with my inner self tells me that I *am* grieving well. I will know joy again." Just remember to be gentle with yourself. Don't add to the negative self-talk by chastising yourself for the voice in the first place; that voice and its messages are a part of who you are in any situation. They simply need the rest of the dialogue, and that's where your personal inner-strength is given a chance to be heard. Don't ignore it.

Allow one confidant: As you find your own way through your grief, consider allowing one other person to walk with you. For many of us, this will be especially difficult. Old tapes about "privacy," "being strong," and "not burdening other people with our problems" try to manipulate us into keeping as much of our grief to ourselves as we possibly can. But we are not wholly private creatures; as human beings, we are creatures born into and fashioned by community. Our problems are not always burdens to others but are often enriching for ourselves and others.

This person need not be some wise guru, a professional counselor, or an ordained minister— although it certainly may be. The person simply needs to be someone you trust, someone who can hear your emotions, respect your experience, and be available to you when the grief rushes in with relentless force. This person needs to honor your tears, allow your anger, celebrate your stories, and invite you to take all the time you need as you grope your way through. If possible, as you ponder who this person might be, look on what you have to share as a gift to the other person; consider how this person will receive a precious part of you and will be so much richer for that which you share.

Seek out a holding environment: A holding environment is a place, experience, or person that allows you to feel safe and taken care of. Don't confuse *safe and taken care of* with *comfortable.* Holding environments can generate discomfort in many ways; the point is, they are safe places in which to be uncomfortable when you need to be.

Perhaps your holding environment is a *place* in nature like a park, the ocean, a lake, or your backyard. Perhaps it's a place where you feel secure with surroundings such as books (a library), works of art (a museum), a specific atmosphere (a church), or certain memories (an old neighborhood). This place may be something as simple and close as a room in your own home.

The *experience* of a holding environment might be a drive in the country where the quiet and wide-open spaces allow you to breathe with greater ease. Perhaps it's watching a sunset, allowing your spirit to sail into the mystery of time changing, days passing. Perhaps your holding experience involves browsing through photo albums, reading, or listening to soothing music—all experiences that open you to hearing sweet and gentle voices that transcend your mind and your thoughts.

Persons can be holding environments to you as well. Perhaps it's the one confidant with whom you've chosen to share your grief journey. It might be a group of people, like a support or prayer group, where your grief is respected and heard. It might be members of a faith community who know the piercing experience of loss, and can participate with you in your darkness because they, too, grieve. In a faith community, you can find the strength of a common belief. Here you can find a holy space into which you can place your questions about "why" and "what now."

Let these places, experiences, and persons be harbors of safety for you, especially when the pain subsides a little. When your heart isn't constricted with grief, it's laid wide open for solace. Give your heart that blessing, then and there, by entering a holding environment.

Ritualize: Ritual is not just an act, something you do; it's a dynamic. You *do* something and that which you do *does something* to you. As you do something relative to your grief, your pain becomes tangible, something your senses can grasp. What you can only feel with your emotions becomes something you can see, touch, taste, hear, smell—the result being that a sense of calm, meaning, and control can return to life.

Develop simple activities that symbolize what you have lost and the fact that you are grieving. If you are a widow, for example, you might want to do something with your wedding band or engagement ring. In an attitude of prayer, you might want to take it off slowly and place it in a sacred place where you'll see it regularly and touch what was and what no longer is. Perhaps you'd want to give it to one of your children or grandchildren, symbolizing the bond of love and life across generations that is not broken with the interruption of death.

If you grieve the change in a relationship, you might want to set aside a regular time to have a mental conversation with that person, imagining what he or she would say in return. In this conversation, you might chat about what brought about the change in the relationship and dream about what the future looks like as you each live with that difference.

Recall the woman who returned to the site of her home that she lost in a fire. That is ritual for her. Every year she returns to that site to remember, to grieve more, and to heal. There, in that place, she can see what she lost and understand what her pain is and what it continues to mean for her year after year. Visiting the gravesite of a loved one, regularly or on special occasions, is this same kind of ritual.

You can give yourself over to these rituals spontaneously, by noting, for example, when a leaf breaks loose from a tree on an autumn afternoon. Watch it float to the ground, and say to yourself, "Yes, that is my experience." Or you can carefully plan your ritual, with attention to time, location, action, and symbols, as I do with my annual visit to my father's grave on the anniversary of his death. With days of prayer anticipating that visit, I relive memories of Dad, I remember the phone call that told me of Dad's heart attack, and I plan what I will take and who I will go with on this particular "pilgrimage."

My friend Mary has a sacred ritual for the anniversary of her mother's death: "Mom loved fresh flowers and gardens of flowers around the house. With a grin on her face, Mom often said to us, 'I want flowers while I'm alive. Don't put them on my grave.' I celebrate the gift of her life each anniversary by giving flowers to someone who can enjoy them."

Bless your memories: As a woman, your memories are precious. They are the golden threads in the fabric of life that help give meaning to your experiences. When you grieve, your memories may seem to be your worst enemies; in fact, they are precious friends. Your memories are like huge chambers where grief can flourish and mature.

Give your grief the opportunity to be full and passionate. When the memories catch you unprepared and off guard, don't fight them. Open up and invite them to come in and be what they need to be, say what they want to say. At the same time, don't wait for these moments to come on their own. Prepare for them and enter them with hope. Set aside time to "go get your memories," and allow yourself to be fully present emotionally to whatever the memories bring. Let them have their own life and their way with you. If they bring pain, then feel the pain; if they bring laughter, smile; if they make you cry, reach for your tissue and stay with the tears. You'll gradually realize how much love and healing you find as you bless your memories and let them have a life of their own that deserves to be heard.

Create a new positive reality: Although by nature you may tend toward optimism or pessimism, you can choose a positive future. The darkness today is certainly real, and it will still be there tomorrow and the next day—and next week and next month. In fact, a part of the darkness will be there for the rest of your life.

But the darkness becomes less massive with time, and you will encounter brief rays of light as you move through your grief. Drawing on your own creative energies, you can catch these brief rays of light by realistically imagining what the other side of darkness will look like. Imagine what you want to feel like and what you want to do someday, when your heart is not so heavy with the void and is more open to the potential. Although this is not the time to act on your imaginings, it is, nonetheless, a time of future-building; pondering a new positive reality is where tomorrow begins, which is part of your grief work.

Draw on your faith traditions: Century upon century of human forming has gone into the evolution of religious traditions. Even the more recently evolved traditions and faith practices have their roots in ancient humanity. These traditions have taken shape out of the daily experiences of life to form expressions that acknowledge something or someone that is bigger than our own experiences of ourselves and of life in general.

Because faith traditions have been fashioned to help us name, celebrate, and be in the midst of Mystery, they embrace all that the human spirit is, as have all these suggestions that focus on spiritual strength. Faith traditions begin with the belief that the human being is a sacred creature endowed by an all-loving Creator with an inner and natural strength (encourage yourself). They are built on the foundation of community (find one confidant), and they name those places (seek out a holding environment) and actions (ritualize) that are sacred. They define the human experience by what has happened (bless your memories), and they foster the critical virtue of hope (create a new, positive reality).

Most faith traditions, for example, have sacred texts that are honored for their wisdom and strength. Consider turning to these Scriptures to hear how they speak to your pain and confusion. Many people, regardless of their own faith traditions, find the Judeo-Christian Scriptures to be a wellspring of solace. There they find the human pain of loss (the Books of Genesis and Exodus), the confusion of unjust suffering (the Book of Job), symphonies of the soul (the Books of Psalms and Proverbs), and the power of hope (the Gospels).

Faith traditions also cultivate certain prayer forms that quiet the noise within so we can hear a Wisdom that is beyond ourselves and our experience. These kinds of prayer are especially powerful when you grieve. Meditation, for example, places the mind in a "clearing" space where you can focus on life minute-by-minute instead of chunk-by-chunk. The repetition of a mantra—a word or phrase, such as *peace, Yahweh,* or *Maranantha (O Lord, come)*—can do the same thing. In that clearing, you are awakened to the depth of your pain as well as the depth of your strength to heal.

The most powerful support offered by a faith tradition is community, where the spiritual, emotional, and physical resources of others make manifest the presence and love of a Higher Power, Creator, God. When you take your grief into the embrace of community, your darkness becomes the doorway through which grace enters the world. In community, you don't have to "be strong," "hide your tears," or "take care of others." Rather, community releases the power of prayer, the strength of emotional understanding and support, and the practical assistance that you need while you grieve.

Note progress: Watch for your own milestones of progress: a memory that does not bring tears, a brief time of prayer that is focused and peaceful, a flush of compassion for another in pain. These simple moments will tell you that the resources of spiritual strength you've been drawing on are, indeed, making you stronger. You are grieving well.

All This as a Woman

- Look at your reflection in a mirror and smile at the person looking back at you. Tell her she is not only capable of grieving well but is, in fact, grieving well.
- Ask yourself, "To whom can I be a gift in the midst of my grief?" Be specific about the qualities you want this person to come away with: respect for your personhood, a sense of humor, patience, perhaps an exposure to the experience of grief.
- What places, experiences, and persons have you turned to in the past to help you celebrate life's joys and support you through life's disappointments? Will any of these be holding environments for you while you grieve?
- Holidays, birthdays, graduations, weddings, funerals all involve ritual. What symbols from these rituals hold potential meaning for you as you ritualize your grief? Candles? Gifts? Ornaments? Flowers?
- How do you define yourself as a woman of faith? How has your faith supported you through major life changes in the past?

The world is round
and the place
which may seem
like the end
may also be only
the beginning.

IVY BAKER PRIEST

You Have the Tools

For women, all life is interrelated. One loss and the grieving we experience in that particular loss will inform, support, and direct another grief. We support ourselves in our own journey through grief by thinking about grief in "safe moments," times when grief is not part of our immediate experience. For example, when I first started work on this book, I asked Bess, my 15-year-old daughter, to tell me about a recent experience of grief for her. She immediately launched into the details surrounding the divorce of friends of ours and how angry she was. She couldn't understand why divorce was the only option and why there had to be so much meanness involved. Because this was a fairly safe topic—our friends' divorce—Bess and I were able to have a healthy discussion about a hard topic. Both of us did a little grief work that night, and someday we will draw on those moments when a harsher grief comes to visit.

I also asked my 27-year-old daughter, Christine, for permission to share with you a few of her thoughts on grief. She willingly and courageously agreed. Listen to how she threads life with death and is aware of grief even in the midst of her great joy:

> *It's really very ironic that life is a series of deaths for me, of me. Each death, each new stage of my life, distances me from one stage and yet endears me and draws me closer to others. For instance, right now, with my recent engagement to Henry, I'm in touch with a lot of grief. I grieve the loss of my life as a single woman. I grieve the fact that the adults in my life can't show me how to do this. I grieve for those in my life who are not 100-percent happy for this choice I am making.*

Thank you, Bess. Thank you, Christine.

Your Grief Tools

In the midst of our grief, we feel like we've lost control of life. We feel like grief has moved in and that, from now on, the pain will be the single most controlling factor in all we do. We feel like we will be at its mercy as it tosses around our emotions and complicates our daily routines.

That is grief. It is powerful enough to *make us*

believe that it will be in control from now on. But it won't, and that's our lifeline of hope. We do get through grief, and we get through well only if we take along with us a belief that we will get through. That belief in ourselves is the single most significant tool we need.

I will never forget the months following my dad's death. My sister and brothers and I all live at considerable distance from one another and from my mother, so ongoing physical support simply wasn't possible. We all had to bid one another farewell after a week of collective grieving, to return to our homes to, more or less, grieve alone. It was a cold and lonely time for all of us.

At one point, I called my sister to see how she was doing, and she seemed remarkably stronger. Through tears, and longing to know some of the peace I was hearing from her across the distance, I asked her: "What's happened, Sheila? You sound so good."

Her voice broke a little, and then she went on to tell me her dream. "Kass, I had a dream about Dad. I dreamed that he and I were driving along in a car. I was driving and we had a flat tire. I steered the car off to the shoulder of the road, we got out, and Dad proceeded to take the jack and spare out of the trunk. I stood off to the side watching, feeling pretty comfortable that Dad would take care of things, as usual. Instead, he placed the equipment on the ground next to the flat and turned to me and said, 'There, now you have all the tools you need to take care of things.' I knew then that I could grieve well, that I was grieving well. I knew I could get through—and that's what I'm doing."

Sheila touched her wisdom in a dream. Some of us will touch that same profound and personal wisdom in something we hear, something we read, something we feel in an unguarded moment. It may visit us when we're in a short span of peace, like the quiet you hear when your car goes under an overpass in a driving rain. It may come to us in the midst of passionate pain, when we scream with all our soul for a way to manage, to cope, just to get through this minute. It may come at us slowly, dawning on us like the arrival of a new day after a long and lonely night.

It will come. Your nature as a woman is grounded in the incredible ability to issue life—especially your own. You have the tools.

For Further Reading

Women in Mourning by Jean Clayton, Omaha: Centering, 1996.

Season of Renewal: A Diary for Women Moving Beyond the Loss of a Love by Judith Finlayson, New York: Crown, 1993.

Necessary Losses: The Loves, Illusions, Dependencies, and Impossible Expectations That All of Us Have to Give Up in Order to Grow by Judith Viorst, New York: Simon & Schuster, 1993.

Life Is Goodbye, Life Is Hello: Grieving Well Through All Kinds of Loss by Alla Renee Bozarth, Ph.D.,Center City, MN: Hazelden, 1982.

How to Survive the Loss of a Love by Melba Colgrove, et. al., Los Angeles: Prelude Press, 1993.

Laugh after Laugh: The Healing Power of Humor by Raymond A. Moody, Jacksonville, FL: Headwaters Press, 1978.

Questions and Answers on Death and Dying by Elisabeth Kubler-Ross, New York: Macmillan, 1974.